WOMAN OF SALT

poems

Beverly Voigt

Los Nietos Press
Downey California
2022

Printed in the United States of America by
Los Nietos Press
Downey, CA 90240
www.LosNietosPress.com
LosNietosPress@gmail.com

Cover photo: "Lot's Wife," courtesy of the artist, Javier Viver (javierviver.com). Life-size sculpture in consolidated salt and wood.

Downtown Pittsburgh Back Cover Photo: Wikipedia User Dllu Used under the Creative Commons Attribution-Share Alike 4.0 International license.
https://creativecommons.org/licenses/by-sa/4.0/deed.en

Point State Park Fountain Photo: Allegheny Conference on Community Development Photographs, Detre Library & Archives Division, Senator John Heinz History Center, Pittsburgh, PA.

Second Edition
ISBN-13: 978-1-7356984-4-1

Originally published by
Seven Kitchens Press, 2018

Contents

to my parents, for their abundant love

WOMAN OF SALT

In the Backyard

We tell our stories wide-eyed
as though we don't believe
them ourselves—how the blue jay

sat among the beans three days
straight and the Vidalia onions
bloomed on strong green stems,

their gauzy bridal caps folding
back, presenting tiny white bouquets.
How she had died on the last day

of spring and what that meant.
How, on the evening of the funeral,
as twilight and the lightning bugs

arrived, and as our grief was just
beginning, two deer—a buck and a doe—
stepped slow and high-footed into the yard,

glowing tawny against the green
silhouette of apple trees. How the buck
moved on to the next yard but the doe

lingered, how she looked up at us
gathered behind the porch railing, then
lowered her head again to the grass.

How she wasn't afraid. How the roses
bloomed so heavy their branches
lay in the dirt.

At the Point View Inn

—Pittsburgh

We have the dining room to ourselves,
the nine adult children, our father,
every in-law and grandchild.

We are in the old Point View Inn
on Brownsville Road, which follows
a Shawnee trail along the highest ridge

above a broad bend of the Monongahela River.
Generals and presidents have stopped here,
countless stagecoaches, and in the cellar,

fugitives from the south on their way
to Canada. My mother is buried in a cemetery
on this same road, a mile out. It has been a week

since her death. But tonight, in this room,
we aren't remembering the bleak hospital
or the crushing funeral. We are all together,

and we are all, somehow, happy. We order pierogies,
chicken sandwiches, fries. The permed waitress,
who knew my mother—who knew everyone—

calls us "hon." We pass plates up and down,
smiling. My sister and I wink and wave
from either end of the long table. Everyone

is somehow shining, as though we've been
rubbed raw. We know now that this
is one of the good times. We will find

our balance. We are on the windward side
of the long Allegheny Front. We are on sandstone
bedrock. We are travelers on this road.

Sumac

As I search for family names, a familiar scent rises
        from the warming woods. Musky, pungent.
I spot its pointed leaves, nodding over the graves
        of infants in tiny plots along the fence.

Inhaling the scent, I am young again,
        at twilight, with my blanket and pillow
on the back porch, watching fireflies slowly enter
        and leave the world. Against clouds

lit orange by the mills I imagine the silhouettes
        of sumac on the next hill to be dragons
breathing the fire of the sky into being, and I fall
        asleep to the train's long rumble along the river.

Like sumac, my family is all over these hills.
        They came for the work and stayed, coming home
year after year from coal hills, barges, mills, with dirty necks
        and soot in their noses, then lay down

for their long sleep beneath this grass. I used to think
        sumac was a neglected weed, a feeling bound up
in my dissatisfaction with these hills, bald
        and bleak for so much of the year. The dirty snow

that hung around the streets too long. The muddy rivers
        with no life to them. A city of blackened buildings.
And I'd wonder at sumac thriving here, bowing
        over the bodies of deer along back roads, blowing dusty

next to passing railcars, clinging to a scattering of earth
        on a ledge of shale, or in the rocky clay soil
of our yard. In fall, the trees would light up, and I'd begin
        to love again, as sumac turned orange

then vermilion, its long stems strung like prayer flags
        across the dying woods. Then winter would swing back,
and I'd hate the sight of their spindly trunks
        on hillsides hung with icicles thick as prison bars.

Now I've reached the oldest tombs, whose mourners
        are long since dead, and I find them neglected, drowning
in overgrowth. I want to read their names but can't get close.
        I see a grave, deep in brush, with a stone coping

formed to hold emblems of love, of promise, of memory.
        And a sapling, spindly and tall, whose scent is as sharp
as its leaves, rises from just where the heart beneath it
        must lie. A new growth that will tolerate the dust

of exhaustion, age and soot, that will thrive here
        as it thrives everywhere, in abandoned train yards,
amid the rusting iron of a steel mill, and in ruined gardens
        full of the roots of other plants.

Slag Pour

—South Hills, Pittsburgh

The sun is borne in a kettle
     to the lip, flaming
          scum of iron, chunks
               of melt, rain

of spark. The kettle
     tips, lets loose its form,
          and a woman of gold floats
               down the gray pile

like a heat-dream, her head
     the remaining fire
          in the throat. More kettles tip and tall
               cinder-women sway

down the heap, in long coats
     and golden babushkas.
          Matryoshki, they nest
               in the hill as it grows, slide

by slide, the alluvial fans
     of their fingers
          spreading against the pile. A pool
               of sun in the bowl

cools, acquires a gray
        skin, a premature moon
                in this still-forming
                        universe. Chain-strung

from a crane, an iron teardrop
        dips to break the skin
                and there is fresh light.
                        The head rolls

as from a guillotine. And the last
        of the women reddens
                to a red star, then
                        pinks. Then

becomes shadow, ash,
        cementitious. Then a darkness
                called night.

Blue Mother

All that long night we hovered,
all of us in the room, watching
her slow retreat. Her feet
so cold, her fingers
going blue.

Again and again
she raised her arm, wanting
out, wanting back.
Again and again, I guided it
down to the bed. All the care
she'd given me, repaid
in such a small gift.

Blue mother in the bed—
Venus in marble—glowing
down that long hallway. Legs
in folds of winding sheets.
One shoulder shrugging off
the world, the other arm
missing, reaching.

I think of the apple tree
in blossom whose branch
I'd once pulled toward me.
Whoa, I whispered, when it reared
in the wind. *I've got you.*

Looking for Life

On a cardboard moon, blue Earth
propped nearby, my mother

pokes her head through the black hole
of an astronaut's helmet and grins.

The camera flash glints off her glasses.
Her hair is just starting its silver turn.

Each morning when the light
comes into my room, I see this photo

and remember her trip with my father
to the space center, where ships have set off

in search of something like ourselves—
on our own shadowed moon, in dry rivulets

on Mars, and lately, in the spumes
of an ice moon caught in a ring of Saturn,

pearl to its oyster. I don't resemble
my mother, but my changes mirror hers

as I reach her age in this photograph,
silver strands in my hair, eyebrows fading.

I look closer, try to remember her voice,
her laugh, her red lips and black hair,

her soft hands. But what am I forgetting?
We lose not just by death but by evaporation

of memory, and by distance—the farther
we look, the more we see only the past.

Pearl moon of Saturn, from which old life
may spring, bring the past forward and show me

my mother again, not at the hour
of her death, but as she was, as I see her

now, in her real, molten life.

Returning to the Dry Garden

After the separation
I return to the desert house

to see what can be salvaged.
Against the garage wall

the pencil plant thrives,
poisonous and greedy.

And the aloe, holding its water
in muscled arms, has sent up

a confident bloom for the hummingbirds.
But the herbs, neglected in my absence,

are lost, their patch of earth stolen
by stringy native weeds.

The violets, campanula with purple bells,
lilac—real lilac—have wilted

in their pots. What took love
and dedicated years

is beyond saving.
I bring the survivors inside

and tend them in the cool kitchen
where I spend afternoons

drinking ice water at the sink
and looking out at a river

that isn't a river, just a channel
for something that rarely comes by.

The Large Cup

When I think of the final months
        I remember the tea

which I knew without asking
        you wanted

I'd bring the large cup
        to your desk at the wall

reach around to embrace you
        kiss your nape

little hollow
        curl of hair

hold my cheek
        next to yours and then

my reward—your warm hand
        on mine

It was all I had left
        this moment that held

no bitterness
        no bite or snap

only the cheek and the nape
        the tea

and the cup
        which I'd wash and provide

wash and provide

Adam in the L.A. River

> *"The mesmerizing surge drew Adam, and like
> other children before him, he slipped into the
> torrent"*
> —*Nancy J. Rigg,* Fire Rescue Magazine

From a local arroyo to the wide cement wash
of the river, he rode rough water, held his head

above the churn, runoff from soil drowned
by unfamiliar rain, destined for debris fields, water

too fast to hope in. News cameras zoomed in
then pulled back suddenly at the terrible details, and he

became ours, this desperate boy, his rough brown hair,
arms outstretched, his familiar, gasping, mouth.

At the Window

A block of sky
A block of beige which is the house

A block of rain
A tiny pane of wooded green

A window caged by iron hearts
soldered point to point

And all at once a bird so swift
the bone behind my tired shoulder

my hidden wing, fast asleep,
jerks to join it

The Lost Sycamore

I know we must carve a living
among the trees. Their roots encroach

on ours, shade our growing food, leave
our chimneys tangle and tinder—

but to slice a sycamore from the earth
whose only crime was to lift an unused sidewalk,

a tree that told the hour by the color of light
on its crown, that encompassed me

at my top-floor window, housed in green light,
that reached so close as to drop leaves

on my porch, leave a dry nest on the eave…
Today men call from the boughs, hold

saws, ropes—actual nooses—and cut piece
from piece this generous tree

that birthed the yellow finch, that sheltered
the brown squirrel, that protected the meal

of the sharp-shinned hawk, and protected me
in my time of need. Tree of solace, of wonder, tree

I lost myself in, tree that regreened my heart.
When the thickest branch fell with echo

and rustle, and the tree reared, losing
its balance, I left the house. I have not yet

examined the stump, only noticed the brighter light
of absence, no recompense, as remnant leaves,

the curled and cracked claws of winter, scuttle
on the porch. Somewhere in the ground

there is a place where nature heals
itself, a taproot to that first spark, a root

that never stops burying itself. I wish
I could set my feet into it, feel that pulse

of water and cells, that essential well
in the green heart of the world, where need

begins, where need is a truth pushing up, always
pushing up, into a new branch, fresh pith,

an unfurling leaf, and dangling seed pods,
rough ornaments of regeneration, just as my heart

is breaking up here in the insufficient air.

Every September

—New York City

In the footprints of the towers,
footlights amplify the night,

two square bodies of light
aimed at the sky

in which moths
fall, flutter, rise, blanched

like souls—no, not
like souls. Remember, I keep

telling myself, the fairies
dreamed up long ago

by two children in a garden,
playing with light

and shadow. Mayflies
they really were, little

human myths light as breath,
with no appetite, no mouths,

and no tomorrows. Yes,
we are given more

than one day—till this day,
when primed for the earth we fall

like heavy fruit, ripe
and sweet. And break

in shadow deeper
than leaf-shade.

Polygon Wood

—A Belgian forest destroyed in the Battle of Ypres, 1917

A farm-carved forest
triangle with one

great wing unfolding—
shredded to stubble

like corn for pigs
Small-arms fire, trees

shoot back, ricochet—
but shellfire

sheers, splinters
This wood

a shadowed breath
What fled, what bound to,

hung from, what
shot against

and how sweet
that wood smelled, oak

and birch, and showers
of leaves in late September

aflame

Sonnet, in Memory

I remember your garage apartment
on Darlington, the kitchen where we played
jazzy love songs, all those things we did at
your table besides eat your scrambled eggs
and cheese. I remember the time we drew
our chairs up to the side window to watch
a summer thunderstorm, let it grow dark
without turning on the lights. Later, when
the rain quieted to a slow drizzle,
I realized you were asleep beside
me for the first time. I thought: I could live
an interior life with you, sitting
at that window, eating at your table,
awake and asleep, letting the light fade.

Earth, Breath

If you stand there, by the yellow deerweed
        after rain
on a morning of gathering heat

the eucalyptus tree above you
        and all it has lost to the mulchy earth
will begin to breathe

and your breath
        remembering itself
will join the exhalation

and the one who is not you
        will evanesce
in the bright air

leaving you in the swing
        of your own
galloping heart

My Conifer

—for a tree stump

In summer
it is warm to the touch.

In winter it seems
primitive

belonging more
to the wood behind

than to the meadow
before it.

Needles fall
among white roots

year after year.

The thing has
shoulders, Venus

against dark pines.
It teaches me to love

what goes cold, what doesn't
come home.

One day
there will be a last visit,

or there already has been.
For now

we are both knitted
like bone to the earth.

In the Passage

—for my mother

In my dreams she is the one sleeping,
in a bed in the rooms I visit, or on a porch,
down a winding hallway, on a mountainside. She
is tucked away, her back to me. I don't try
to wake her, I just ask the ex-boyfriend,
or the maharajah, or the sumac tree I'm dreaming of
to keep it down. It is when I begin to wake
that I hear her calling me, or her call begins
to wake me. And I am a child again, and she's
downstairs, calling up to say it's time
for supper, or to bring down my dirty clothes.
Or to tell me she's going out and when
she'll be back. I want to respond from the top
of the stairs, *See you soon*, run down
and hug her, kiss her soft cheek, before
she crosses that threshold. I want to stay here,
in this passage, this warm half-sleep, where she is,
where she still is. Or just her voice, which
I would accept as enough, as a gift from whatever
rules the unconscious, the gift of my memory
of her, coming back in the door. But the day
is dragging me across its brink, into bright light
and cares, into another day empty of her. These
ten years. And she is still below, calling me.
Her voice like a bell.

Pittsburgh: The Fourth River

An underground river, aquifer of memory,
cistern of ancient lake that runs beneath
these three seen rivers, triangle of history

and hope, is pushed, rushed to the point, to
the Point, and carves, emerges, juts into this pool,
in which I am fifteen, wading, a new river flowing

in me as well, with friends down from our hill-perch
among carved stones to this opening day, this circle
of new stone, wide plateau of water, and its first gush

into air. Girl of sulfurous mornings, toast
and smoke in my mouth, I descended hollows ringing
with locust screams, the green around me alive, shimmering,

crossed ahead of a train groaning a curve
to the metal city, awake, ringing of hot pour and transport,
trestle and underpinning, and then the green gorge

of the river. There is big sky here you can't see
from the enveloping hills, these Alleghenies, an openness
that sets forth, to bigger, to wider, to the Ohio,

to the Gulf. Girl of pen and broken sidewalk.
Of unflowered heart. I watched those tallest buildings rise
above our hilltop and peer down our alleys

like blinkered giants. Woman of salt, I looked back
on that dying city, its destruction, rusted metal, open grates
of sumac—oh exile, weeks of dark rain, damp newspapers,

then the great forgetting. Now, woman of bruised hands
dark as tulip petals, I stand here again. Freshened rivers cut
through valley and moraine. The bruised land cleanses

itself, recovers, even within my own lifetime. I know
it can be done. Something about how old these mountains,
these Appalachians, how high they once reached.

What can be carved, and what just takes time. From the river
that worms below like a promise, a reflection
of goodness in the landscape. In what was tenement, now

testament. I watch dark birds wash themselves, over
and over, in those great shallows. I know it can be done.

Fountain at Point State Park, 1974

Notes & Acknowledgments

"Blue Mother" appeared as a Cross-Tie at the website of *West Trestle Review,* Oct. 27, 2015.

"In the Backyard" won the 2008 Friends of Acadia Poetry Prize (judged by Wesley McNair) and appeared in *Friends of Acadia Journal,* Summer/Fall 2008, vol. 15, no. 2.

"Looking for Life" appeared in *Crab Creek Review,* Fall 2015.

"Sonnet, in Memory" appeared as Poem of the Month at Terry Wolverton's Writers at Work website, June 2012.

About the Author

Beverly Voigt is a native of Pittsburgh, Pennsylvania. She works as an editor and layout specialist in the South Bay area of Los Angeles. A Pushcart Prize nominee, Beverly has had poems published in *Crab Creek Review, Friends of Acadia Journal, Sonora Review,* and elsewhere. Her second chapbook, *Song of the Overcast,* was released in February 2022 from Finishing Line Press.